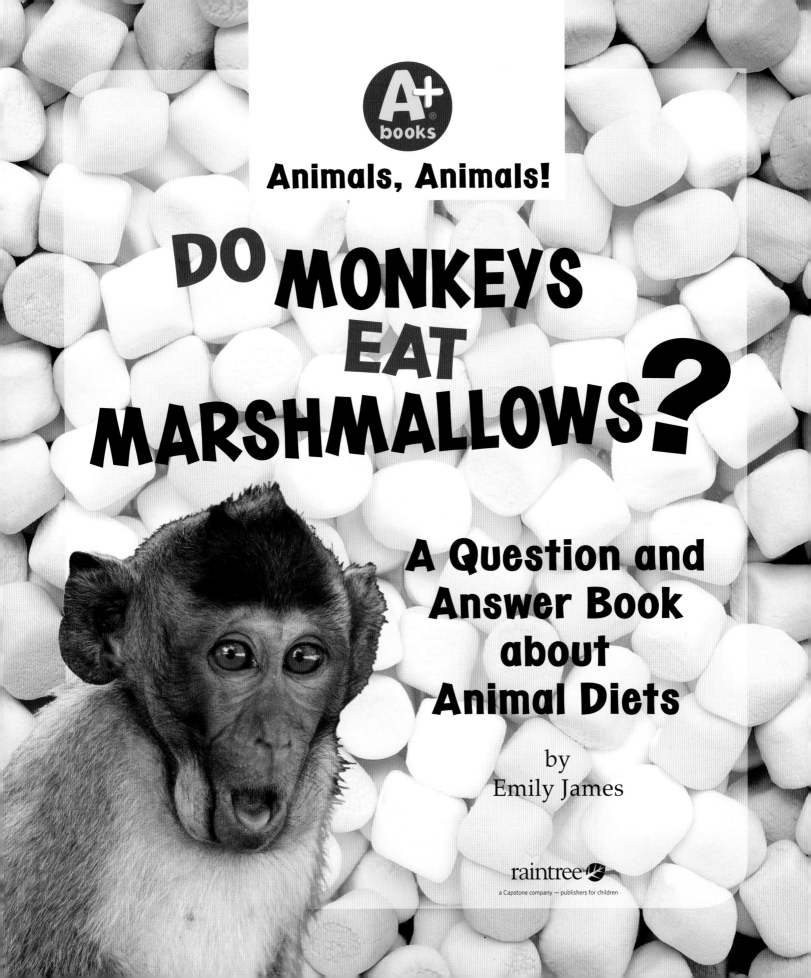

A⁺ books

Animals, Animals!

DO MONKEYS EAT MARSHMALLOWS?

A Question and Answer Book about Animal Diets

by
Emily James

raintree

a Capstone company — publishers for children

Raintree is an imprint of Capstone Global Library Limited, a company incorporated in England and Wales having its registered office at 264 Banbury Road, Oxford, OX2 7DY – Registered company number: 6695582

www.raintree.co.uk

myorders@raintree.co.uk

Edited by Jaclyn Jaycox
Designed by Juliette Peters
Picture research by Jo Miller
Production by Laura Manthe

ISBN 978 1 4747 2793 8
20 19 18 17 16
10 9 8 7 6 5 4 3 2 1

BRITISH LIBRARY CATALOGUING IN PUBLICATION DATA
A full catalogue record for this book is available from the British Library.

PHOTO CREDITS
iStockphoto: Peopleimages, 26; Minden Pictures: Katherine Feng, 22 (inset); Newscom: Arco Images G/picture alliance/Delpho, M., 20, 27 (top); Shutterstock: AngleArt, 24, Avirut Somsam, 12, belizar, 28 (top), Cloud7Days, cover (marshmallows), David Dirga, 4, David Ryo, 22, Ewais, 10, Ferderic B, 14, fontoknak, 1, back cover, Henk Paul, 28 (bottom), Jean-Edouard Rozey, 18, Karel Gallas, 16, Moize nicolas, 6, Naypong, 32, PyTy, 8, Ryan M. Bolton, cover (monkey), Volodymyr Goinyk, 27 (bottom)

Design Elements:
Shutterstock: AN NGUYEN, djgis

Printed in China.

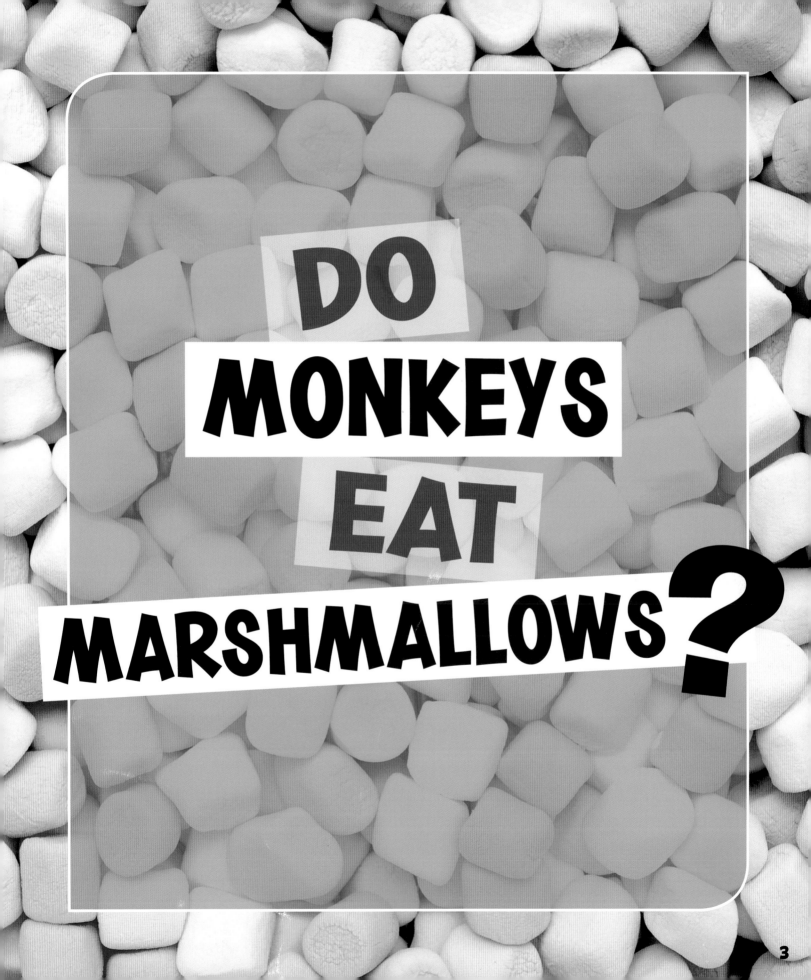

DO MONKEYS EAT MARSHMALLOWS?

No! Monkeys eat mangoes.

Monkeys scramble up fruit trees. They pluck sweet mangoes and tear them open. Monkeys also eat leaves and flowers. Even a frog, lizard, bat or insect might become a monkey's meal.

DO SHARKS EAT MARSHMALLOWS?

No! Sharks eat fish.

Sharks are giant ocean fish that eat smaller fish. Sharks have five to 15 rows of sharp teeth that can bite through bone.

DO GIRAFFES EAT MARSHMALLOWS?

No! Giraffes eat leaves.

Giraffes stretch their long necks to reach the branches of tall trees. They nibble at the leaves. A giraffe's tongue can slip between thorny branches. It can twist around a tasty bud.

DO COWS EAT MARSHMALLOWS?

No! Cows eat grass.

Cows graze on grass in green meadows. They also eat clover, peas, corn and hay. Cows chew and swallow their food. They bring it up later to chew it again. This is called chewing the cud.

DO RABBITS EAT MARSHMALLOWS?

No! Rabbits eat carrots.

Pet rabbits eat carrots as a special treat.
Wild rabbits eat mostly green, leafy plants.
But in winter green leaves are scarce.
Hungry rabbits eat twigs and tree bark.

DO ORCAS EAT MARSHMALLOWS?

No! Orcas eat squid.

Orcas are good hunters. Besides slippery squid, orcas eat fish, turtles and seals. They even eat seabirds when they can catch them.

DO ANTEATERS EAT MARSHMALLOWS?

No! Anteaters eat ants.

Anteaters rip open anthills with their sharp claws. Their long, sticky tongues snatch up the scurrying ants. An anteater's tongue can worm its way deep into ant tunnels.

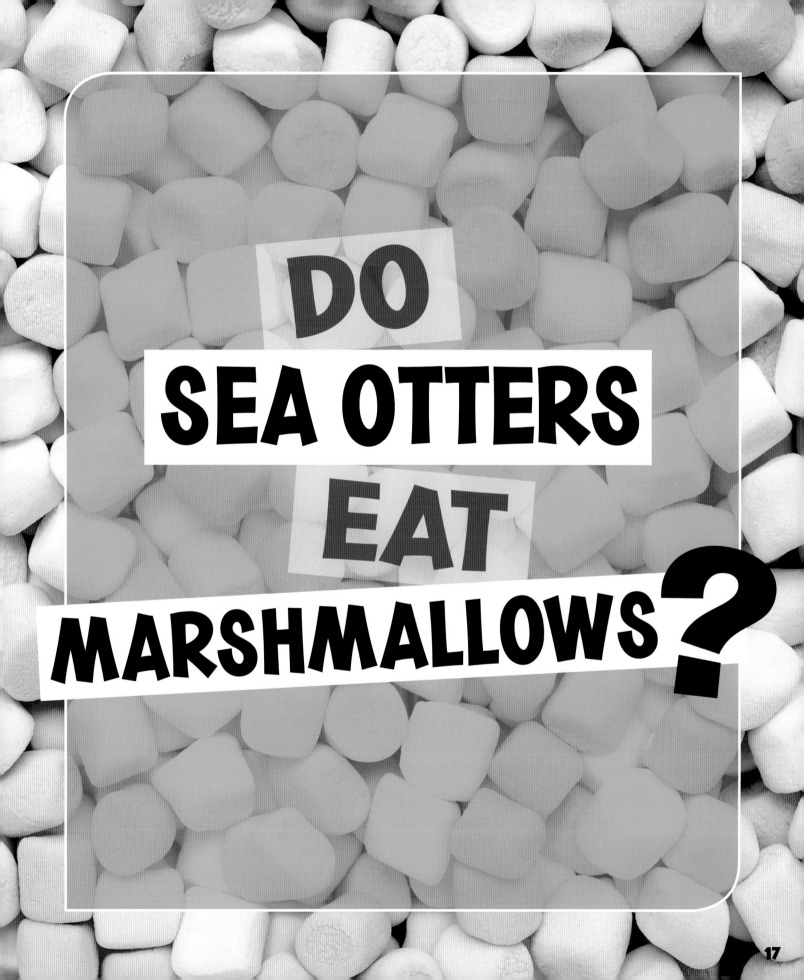

DO SEA OTTERS EAT MARSHMALLOWS?

No! Sea otters eat crabs.

Sea otters dive to the ocean floor to find food.
They eat crabs, sea urchins, clams, fish and snails.
Sea otters bring their food to the water's surface.
They eat while floating on their backs.

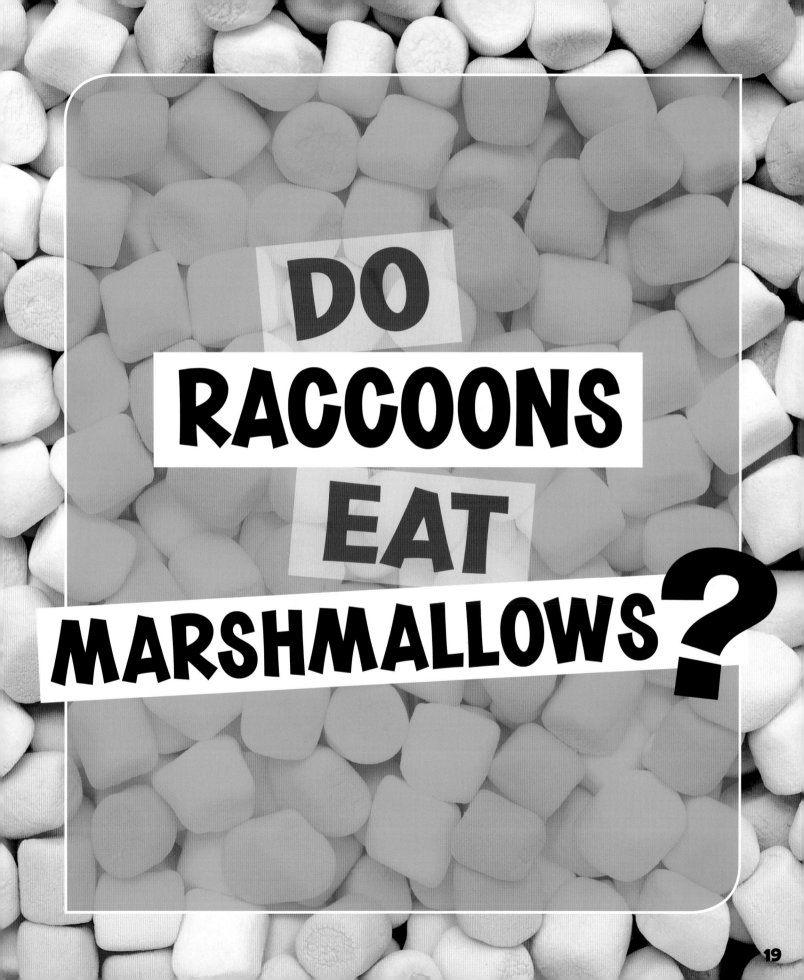

DO RACCOONS EAT MARSHMALLOWS?

No! Raccoons eat berries.

Raccoons ramble through bushes, picking berries with their paws. They also eat seeds, nuts, eggs and fruit. Raccoons eat more food in the autumn to pack on extra fat for winter.

DO PANDAS EAT MARSHMALLOWS?

No! Pandas eat bamboo.

Pandas have special front paws with bony thumbs. The thumbs are good for gripping stiff bamboo stems. Powerful panda jaws and teeth chew through the stems and tough roots.

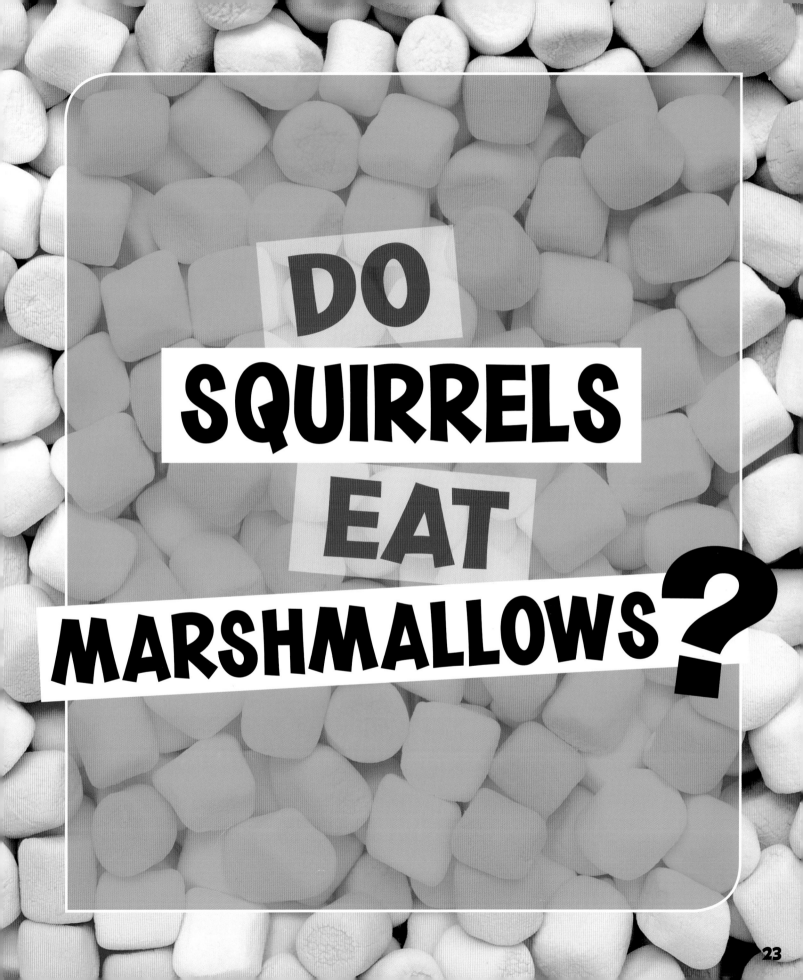

DO SQUIRRELS EAT MARSHMALLOWS?

No! Squirrels eat nuts.

Squirrels scamper through trees and leap from branch to branch. They search for food on the ground. Squirrels eat acorns, nuts, berries and insects. They have sharp front teeth that never stop growing.

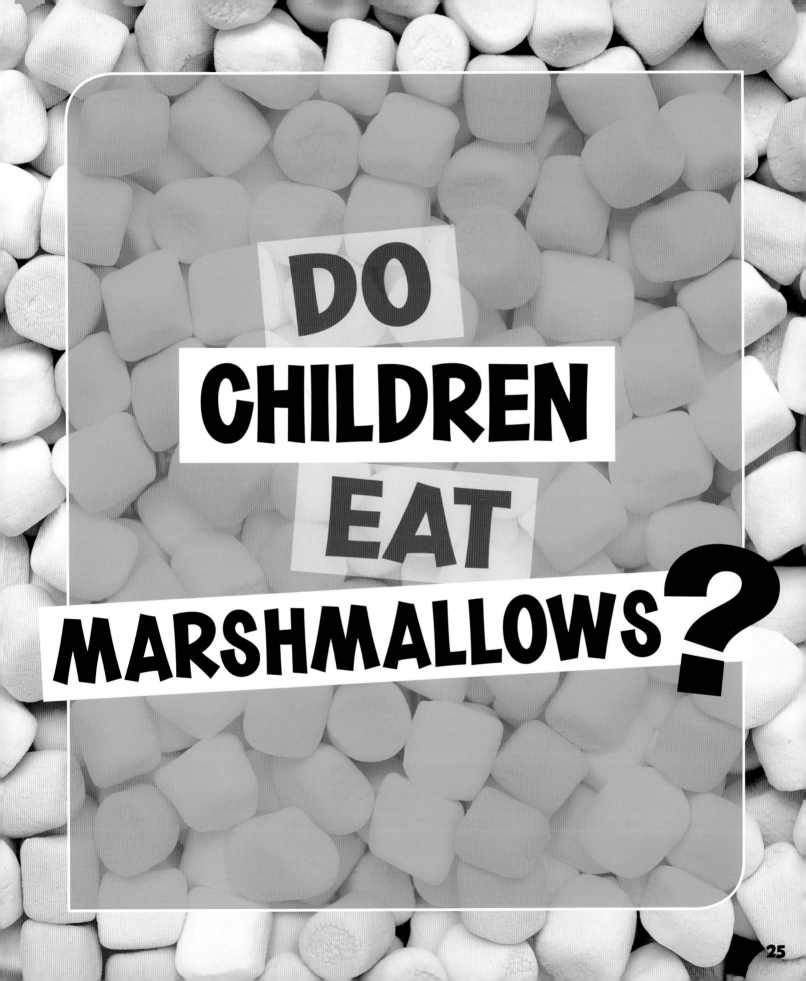

DO CHILDREN EAT MARSHMALLOWS?

Yes! Children eat marshmallows.

Children eat vegetables and bread. They eat fruit and meat too. Children eat many of the same foods that animals eat. Children eat food cooked on the hob or baked in the oven. For a special treat, children might even eat marshmallows roasted over a fire!

Animal diets

Animals eat soft things.

tangy berries ⟶ raccoons
squishy mangoes ⟶ monkeys
green grass ⟶ cows

Animals eat hard things.

tough bamboo ⟶ pandas
crispy carrots ⟶ rabbits
crunchy nuts ⟶ squirrels

Raccoons love to eat berries.

a hungry panda eating bamboo

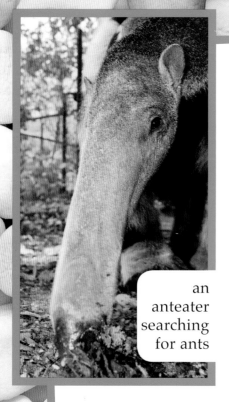

an anteater searching for ants

Animals eat things that wiggle and move.

slippery fish ⟶ sharks
squishy squid ⟶ orcas
creepy-crawly ants ⟶ anteaters
snappy crabs ⟶ sea otters

a giraffe eating leaves

Animals eat food that grows up high.

tasty leaves on tall, tall trees ⟶ giraffes

GLOSSARY

anthill nest built by ants in the shape of a mound

bamboo tall, woody type of grass with hard, hollow stems

bud tightly closed flower or leaf that has not yet opened

clover small, leafy plants that grow low to the ground

cud partly chewed and swallowed food that a cow brings up again to chew some more

scarce hard to find. Leaves on trees are scarce during winter.

sea urchin sea creature with a hard, spiny shell. The spines are used for protection and also help the sea urchin move around.

squid sea animal with a long, soft body and 10 finger-like arms used to grasp food

COMPREHENSION QUESTIONS

1. Which animal's front teeth never stop growing?
2. Pandas use their strong jaws and teeth to chew bamboo. What is bamboo?
3. What kinds of food does your favourite animal eat?

READ MORE

Do Mice Eat Rice?, Al Wight (Tuttle Publishing, 2012

How and What Do Animals Eat? (All About Animals Close-Up), Bobbie Kalman (Crabtree Publishing Company, 2015)

What Do Animals Eat? (Little Book of Answers), Ruby Maile (Three Crows Media, 2013)

WEBSITES

www.bbc.co.uk/education/clips/zwfd2p3
This video clip explores what different animals eat.

www.ngkids.co.uk/animals
Learn amazing facts about animals on this website.

www.sciencekids.co.nz/gamesactivities/teetheating.html
In this game you'll learn why animals have different kinds of teeth.

LOOK FOR ALL THE BOOKS IN THE SERIES

DO COWS HAVE KITTENS?
A Question and Answer Book about Animal Babies

DO GOLDFISH FLY?
A Question and Answer Book about Animal Movements

DO MONKEYS EAT MARSHMALLOWS?
A Question and Answer Book about Animal Diets

DO WHALES HAVE WHISKERS?
A Question and Answer Book about Animal Body Parts

INDEX